A BUSINESS APPROACH TO SPINACH FARMING

Complete Entrepreneurial Step By Step Guide To Spinach Garden From Scratch

ZHURI HART

DISCLAIMER

This book is intended to provide general information and insights on adopting a business approach to farming. The content within is based on the author's knowledge and experiences up to the date of publication. It is essential to recognize that the field of agriculture is dynamic, influenced by various factors such as market conditions, climate, and regulatory changes.

Readers are advised to conduct thorough research, seek professional advice, and consider their unique circumstances before implementing any strategies or practices discussed in this book. The author and publisher disclaim any responsibility for the accuracy, completeness, or suitability of the information provided. The book is not a substitute for professional advice, and the author and publisher shall not be liable for any damages or losses arising from the use or reliance on the information presented herein.

Individual results may vary, and success in farming enterprises is contingent upon numerous variables. The author encourages readers to consult with relevant experts, agricultural extension services, and legal or financial professionals to tailor strategies to their specific needs and local conditions.

This book is not intended to be a comprehensive guide to all aspects of farming, and readers should exercise their judgment and discretion in applying the principles discussed. The author and publisher do not endorse any specific products, services, or companies mentioned in this book unless explicitly stated.

By reading this book, the reader acknowledges and accepts the inherent uncertainties in agricultural endeavors and agrees to use the information at their own risk.

TABLE OF CONTENTS

ABOUT THE BOOK

For those looking to start and run profitable spinach farming operation, this extensive manual, "A Business Approach to Spinach Farming," is a priceless tool. The book starts with a thoughtful summary of spinach growing, emphasizing how important it is for the agricultural industry to embrace a business-oriented strategy. By exploring the book's main goals, readers can comprehend the direction and goal of the work with clarity.

The book establishes the framework by explaining the botanical history, range of variations, nutritional value, and requirements for soil and climate unique to spinach. Having this knowledge helps you make well-informed decisions at every step of growing spinach. The significance of market research and demand analysis is emphasized strategically. Readers are guided through the process of identifying target clients, evaluating market trends, and analyzing the demand for spinach products.

A key component of long-term success in the spinach farming sector is alignment with market trends, which is ensured by this data-driven strategy.

The book offers helpful advice on how to build a spinach farm. It covers topics like creating a business strategy, choosing a location, getting the property ready, and incorporating the right machinery and technology. Cultivation strategies, such as seed selection, germination, planting, spacing, irrigation systems, fertilizer, soil management, ideal harvesting times, and post-harvest management, are covered in detail. These sections give readers the fundamental knowledge and abilities required for productive spinach farming and preserving product quality.

Beyond cultivation, the book examines important commercial elements. To increase market reach and profitability, its discussion of marketing tactics emphasizes the significance of branding, packaging, presentation, distribution networks, and price strategies.

In-depth information on cost analysis, budgeting, financial planning, and funding possibilities unique to spinach farming is provided, which explores financial management. It guides readers through legal and regulatory matters, including how to comprehend agricultural rules, secure the required licenses and permissions, and guarantee environmental standards are met.

"A Business Approach to Spinach Farming" provides a comprehensive manual that skillfully combines the science of business management with the art of growing spinach, equipping would-be farmers with the information and abilities necessary to build a successful and long-lasting farm.

CHAPTER ONE

SPINACH FARMING INTRODUCTION

AN OVERVIEW OF FARMING SPINACH

The cultivation of spinach, a leafy green vegetable prized for its nutritional content and adaptability in a wide range of culinary applications, is known as spinach farming. As a member of the amaranth family, spinach is a popular option for consumers who are health-conscious because it is high in vitamins, minerals, and antioxidants. Spinach is cultivated in a variety of climates and locales, with distinct kinds suiting diverse environmental requirements.

Preparing the soil, planting the seeds, irrigating it, managing pests, and harvesting the crop are all important phases in the production of spinach. To maximize the quantity and quality of spinach crops, farmers need to take into account variables including climate, soil quality, and water availability.

To increase the productivity of spinach production and lessen its negative environmental effects, modern farming methods including hydroponics and greenhouse cultivation have also been used.

THE VALUE OF A BUSINESS STRATEGY

It is impossible to exaggerate the significance of using a business strategy when growing spinach. Although farming has always been thought of as a means of subsistence or a means of support, approaching the industry from a commercial standpoint offers a strategic viewpoint that can result in long-term success. Adopting technologies that can increase productivity and efficiency, managing risks, and carefully planning are all necessary components of putting good business practices into practice when growing spinach.

A business strategy for spinach farming places a strong emphasis on the necessity of market research to comprehend customer preferences; spot industry trends, and create a competitive advantage.

This method entails drafting a business plan that includes financial predictions, strategies, and goals. To properly position their spinach products in the market, farmers must take into account variables including pricing, distribution routes, and branding.

Moreover, an essential component of the company strategy is incorporating ecologically friendly and sustainable practices into the spinach farming process. This entails using resources sensibly, producing as little waste as possible and using methods that support biodiversity and soil health.

In addition to being in line with customer tastes, sustainable farming supports the long-term profitability of the spinach-growing industry.

In summary, a variety of techniques are used in spinach cultivation to produce this nutrient-dense leafy green. Since a commercial approach incorporates market orientation, strategic thinking, and sustainability considerations, it is essential for the success of spinach farming endeavors.

A crucial factor in the dynamic and changing agricultural sector is spinach farming with a commercial approach, as the need for sustainable and healthful food options grows.

CHAPTER TWO

COMPREHENDING SPINACH

BACKGROUND IN BOTANY

The leafy green vegetable spinach, scientifically known as Spinacia oleracea, is prized for its abundance of nutrients and is a member of the Amaranthaceae family. The crinkly, dark green leaves of this annual plant are affixed to succulent stems. Usually, a plant's life cycle lasts one year, at which point it stops growing and produces seeds. Known for its adaptability and versatility, spinach grows well in a wide range of soil types and temperatures around the world. Its botanical qualities make it a perfect crop for growing and eating, which adds to its widespread appeal as a mainstay in many different cuisines across the globe.

DIFFERENT TYPES OF SPINACH

There are numerous types of spinach, each with distinct qualities that suit varying tastes and cultivation circumstances. Savoy spinach is a popular choice in salads and cooking because of its strong texture and crinkly leaves. In contrast, smooth-leafed or flat-leafed spinach has smoother leaves and is preferred for ease of preparation and washing. Baby spinach is a popular ingredient in salads and smoothies since it is collected early in the growing season and is valued for its mild flavor and suppleness. Another spinach type prized for taste and appearance is Bloomsdale, which has dark green, savoy leaves. Because there are so many different spinach types, growers and consumers can customize their selections according to environmental factors, culinary applications, and taste preferences.

VALUE NUTRITIONALLY

Hailed as a nutritional powerhouse, spinach is a great source of important vitamins, minerals, and antioxidants. It is a great source of vitamins A and C, which are essential for healthy skin and a strong immune system. Furthermore, spinach has a high iron content, which helps to produce hemoglobin and prevents anemia. For the production and repair of DNA, spinach contains folate, which is especially important during times of fast cell division. This leafy green is also low in calories and carbs, which makes it a great option for people trying to keep their weight in check.

The nutritional composition of spinach includes elements like calcium, magnesium, and potassium that support several body processes, including bone and muscle health. Spinach's rich supply of antioxidants, including lutein and zeaxanthin, lowers the risk of age-related macular degeneration and improves eye health. Given all of these benefits, spinach is a great addition to a diet that is both nutrient-rich and well-balanced.

CONDITIONS OF THE SOIL AND CLIMATE

Because of its extraordinary climate adaptation, spinach is a crop that can be grown in a variety of conditions. Spinach may grow in both the spring and the fall, though it favors cool weather. It's important to remember that excessive heat might induce spinach to bolt, a condition in which the plant develops blossoms and seeds before its time, which affects the quality of the leaves. As a result, gardeners frequently concentrate on scheduling the planting of spinach to protect it from harsh weather.

When it comes to soil requirements, spinach prefers soil that drains well and is high in organic matter. For best growth, a pH range of slightly acidic to neutral. Fertile soils are ideal for spinach plants, and adding compost or other organic matter can improve the soil's nutrient content and structure. Especially during dry spells, the soil must have enough moisture, thus regular watering techniques should be used to keep it from drying out. A plentiful harvest of nutrient-dense spinach leaves can be guaranteed by cultivators by comprehending and fulfilling certain climate and soil needs.

CHAPTER THREE

DEMAND ANALYSIS AND MARKET RESEARCH

EVALUATING CURRENT MARKET TRENDS

Market trends have a significant impact on how businesses operate, and making well-informed decisions requires a careful analysis of them. It entails the methodical analysis of changes in consumer behavior, innovations in technology, the state of the economy, and other outside variables that might affect the market. Businesses can foresee changes and respond proactively to new possibilities or obstacles by keeping an eye on these patterns. Understanding trends in sustainability, dietary changes, and health and wellness can help understand consumer expectations and preferences when it comes to spinach products.

DETERMINING THE TARGET MARKET

Developing an effective marketing strategy starts with identifying your target audience. This calls for a thorough comprehension of the ideal consumer's behavioral, psychographic, and demographic traits. When it comes to spinach products, age, dietary preferences, lifestyle decisions, and cultural norms are important considerations. By doing market segmentation, companies can better target particular consumer categories with their products and marketing initiatives, increasing the efficacy of their outreach. Businesses can deploy resources more effectively and produce a persuasive message that appeals to potential customers by narrowing in on their target demographic.

EVALUATING PRODUCT DEMAND FOR SPINACH

Demand for spinach products is analyzed using a complex methodology that considers several variables that affect consumer behavior. First and foremost, evaluating the nutritional content and health advantages of spinach is essential since this data has a big impact on consumer demand. Furthermore, it's critical to comprehend the competitive environment and the distinct advantages of spinach products over rivals. To determine the present and future demand for spinach products, market research should examine consumer attitudes, preferences, and purchase behaviors. To guarantee a thorough grasp of the market dynamics, seasonal variations, regional preferences, and cultural considerations should also be taken into account in this study. Businesses can adjust their manufacturing, marketing, and distribution strategies to meet and capitalize on consumer needs by understanding the variables driving demand.

Demand analysis and market research are essential parts of a strategic company plan. Through the evaluation of market trends, target client identification, and demand analysis for spinach goods, firms may obtain a comprehensive picture of their market environment. They may use this information to improve their offers, make well-informed decisions, and maintain an advantage in a market that is always changing and highly competitive.

CHAPTER FOUR

ORGANIZING YOUR FARM TO GROW SPINACH

CREATING A BUSINESS STRATEGY

To guarantee a prosperous and long-lasting enterprise, meticulous evaluation of multiple aspects is necessary while organizing a spinach farm. The creation of an extensive business plan is a vital step in this planning process. A well-written business plan outlines your objectives, tactics, and projected financials, acting as a guide. It is an essential tool for drawing in investors, getting financing, and helping you make decisions that will affect your spinach farm for the duration of its existence.

Understanding the need for spinach in your target market is crucial information to have in your business plan, so make sure to investigate it thoroughly. Examine market trends, competitive analysis, and potential obstacles. Your pricing strategy, marketing technique, and unique selling proposition should all be clearly stated in your business plan. It should also include your sales and production projections so you can create reasonable deadlines and targets.

SELECTING A SITE AND PREPARING THE LAND

Planning an effective spinach farm requires careful consideration of both site selection and land preparation. Select a growing area for spinach that has enough drainage, sun exposure, and soil quality. Test the soil to determine pH and nutrient levels and to make sure the growing conditions are ideal. To reduce logistical issues, take into account the markets' and the transportation facilities' proximity. Clearing, plow work, and soil leveling are examples of adequate site preparation that produce a favorable growing environment for spinach.

TOOLS AND TECHNOLOGY

Your spinach farm's productivity and efficiency greatly depend on the technology and equipment you use.

Invest in irrigation systems, plows, and tractors as well as other contemporary farming equipment to increase yields and streamline operations. Accept technology for jobs like temperature, crop health, and soil moisture monitoring.

Precision farming has the potential to reduce environmental impact while optimizing resource utilization. Keep up with developments in agricultural technology to maintain your farm's competitiveness and long-term viability.

Growing spinach requires efficient irrigation, and the sort of irrigation system you use relies on several variables, including climate, soil composition, and water availability. For example, drip irrigation is renowned for its accurate distribution of water to the root zones of plants and its high efficiency. Appropriate irrigation system implementation can enhance crop production and conserve water.

Careful planning is the cornerstone of a prosperous spinach farm. A key part of this planning process is creating a thorough business strategy, picking the farm site with care, and making the necessary investments in technology and equipment. You may start a spinach farm that is not only profitable but also environmentally and economically sustainable if you take these factors into account.

CHAPTER FIVE

METHODS OF CULTIVATION
SELECTION AND GERMINATION OF SEEDS

Because it directly affects the quality and productivity of the crops, seed selection is an essential part of the agricultural process. When selecting seeds, farmers need to take into account variables including the intended purpose, soil type, and climate.

Due to their superior qualities, such as increased yields and disease resistance, hybrid varieties are frequently chosen. The process via which a seed becomes a seedling is called germination. Sufficient moisture, warmth, and oxygen are necessary for effective germination.

Utilizing methods such as scarification or stratification, farmers can increase germination rates and give their plants a head start.

PLANTING AND ARRANGEMENT

Effective planting methods have a major role in the overall success of farming. The crop type and regional conditions determine the best planting technique, whether it be transplanting or direct seeding. For the best possible air circulation, nutrient absorption, and sunlight exposure, plants must be spaced appropriately apart. Plant density influences crop yield overall as well as the development of individual plants. The right planting spacing depends on several aspects that farmers must take into account, including the crop's intended purpose, the mature size of the plants, and their root systems.

TECHNIQUES FOR IRRIGATION

Managing water well is crucial to the health and yield of crops. Different crop varieties and environmental conditions are catered to by a variety of irrigation techniques, including flood irrigation, sprinkler systems, and drip irrigation.

For example, drip irrigation minimizes water waste and lowers the risk of illness by delivering water directly to the plant roots. The kind of soil, the climate, and the availability of water are all important considerations for farmers when choosing the best irrigation technique. From germination to maturity, a plant's life cycle depends on regular and sufficient moisture.

MANAGING SOIL AND FERTILIZATION

One of the most important ways to provide crops with the nutrients they need for healthy growth is through fertilization. Both synthetic and organic fertilizers have advantages and things to consider when used by farmers. To preserve the health of the soil, soil management techniques include conservation tillage, cover crops, and crop rotation.

For plants to absorb nutrients, the pH and nutrient levels of the soil must be appropriate. Farmers must routinely evaluate the state of their soil, do soil tests, and modify their fertilization plans as necessary.

Long-term soil fertility and health are enhanced by sustainable practices including the addition of cover crops and the usage of organic matter.

CONTROL OF PESTS AND DISEASES

A successful harvest depends on protecting crops from pests and diseases. Biological, cultural, and chemical control techniques are combined in integrated pest management (IPM) programs. IPM cultural methods include things like crop rotation, companion planting, and the introduction of beneficial insects. To enable prompt response, farmers should periodically inspect their fields for symptoms of disease and pests. Pesticide application is one example of a chemical control technique that should be used sparingly to reduce its negative effects on the environment. Furthermore, breeding or genetic modification can help create crop varieties resistant to pests, which can support sustainable pest management techniques. For pest and disease control in cultivation to be efficient, regular scouting and early identification are still essential.

CHAPTER SIX

HARVESTING AND MANAGING AFTER HARVEST

IDEAL TIMES FOR HARVESTING

A crucial component of agriculture that directly affects crop quality and output is figuring out when to harvest. The type of crop, the weather, and the intended purpose all influence the best time to harvest. Timing is critical for many commodities, including fruits and vegetables, to guarantee optimal flavor, nutritional value, and overall market worth.

To determine when to harvest, farmers frequently use visual signals including color, size, and maturity indicators. To meet market expectations and enhance produce quality, elements including ripeness and shelf life must be balanced. In addition to improving the nutritional value and flavor, timely harvesting reduces losses from spoiling or overripening.

AFTER-HARVEST MANAGEMENT AND PRESERVATION

Harvested crops' shelf life and quality are greatly increased by proper post-harvest treatment and storage. It's important to handle properly in the first several days following harvesting, as poor handling can cause large losses. Sorting, washing, and packing are examples of proper handling techniques used to get rid of tainted or damaged food.

Maintaining ideal storage conditions and shielding crops from physical harm require effective packaging. Depending on the crop's perishability and type, different storage techniques apply. Common methods to slow down the natural degradation processes are cold storage, controlled environment storage, and refrigeration.

Using suitable handling and storage procedures after harvest guarantees that the produce reaches consumers with little loss and maintains its nutritious content.

MEASURES FOR QUALITY CONTROL

For agricultural products to remain marketable and up to standards in the post-harvest period, quality control methods are essential. These precautions cover a variety of tasks, such as routine inspections, sorting, and applying hygienic procedures.

Evaluating characteristics including size, color, form, and defect-free status are examples of inspection criteria. The application of food safety regulations is a part of quality control as well, guaranteeing that the harvested produce is free of pollutants and dangerous diseases.

Using contemporary technologies, such as imaging systems and sensors, can help identify flaws and guarantee consistency in quality.

For fruit to stay fresh and avoid spoiling, regular monitoring of temperature, humidity levels, and storage conditions is essential.

Ensuring the sustainability of agricultural companies and meeting consumer expectations and regulatory requirements require the integration of thorough quality control procedures into the post-harvest management process.

CHAPTER SEVEN

MARKETING TECHNIQUES

BRANDING YOUR SPINACH FARM

Building a strong brand for your spinach farm is essential to building a reputation in the marketplace. Determine the special selling points of your spinach, such as its organic origin, local sourcing, or sustainable farming methods. Create a brand narrative that is appealing to customers and distinguishes your spinach from rivals. Think about coming up with a catchy logo and producing eye-catching packaging that captures the spirit of your company. Developing a brand identity that is consistent with the beliefs of your intended market can encourage a close bond and steadfast devotion.

PRESENTATION & PACKAGING

Your spinach presentation is crucial to drawing customers in and setting it out from the competition on the shelf. Choose packaging that is aesthetically pleasing in addition to being useful in maintaining freshness. Make use of environmentally friendly materials to satisfy the increasing demands of customers for sustainability. Important information like nutritional data, certifications, and the history of the farm must be communicated through labels that are understandable and educational.

Putting money on visually appealing designs can improve the way your food is presented overall, making it stand out and encouraging customers to pick it over competing products.

DISTRIBUTION CHANNELS

Selecting the appropriate distribution channels is essential to guaranteeing that your spinach effectively reaches its intended market. Investigate a variety of distribution channels, such as Internet platforms, restaurants, grocery shops, and local farmers' markets. Forming alliances with nearby merchants will aid in spreading the word about your spinach in the neighborhood, and working with internet marketplaces will enable you to reach a larger market. Furthermore, contemplate introducing a direct-to-consumer business strategy that enables clients to buy spinach straight from your farm via internet sales platforms or subscription services, creating a more intimate relationship between your company and its customers.

STRATEGIES FOR PRICING

When choosing a price strategy for your spinach, it's important to take perceived value, market demand, and manufacturing costs into account. To determine a starting point for pricing, thoroughly examine all of your production costs, including those associated with planting, harvesting, and packaging. To comprehend the pricing trends in your industry and area, think about conducting market research.

Offering clients options while optimizing revenue can be achieved by implementing tiered pricing or bundling options. Incorporating discounts or promotions at busy times of the year can also boost sales and instill a sense of urgency among customers. Remaining profitable while maintaining competitive pricing is necessary for long-term success in the spinach market.

CHAPTER EIGHT

ANALYSIS OF FINANCIAL MANAGEMENT

EXPENSES

An essential component of financial management is cost analysis, which is assessing and comprehending all of the costs related to a specific project or line of business. Cost analysis in the context of spinach farming financial management would include a thorough examination of both direct and indirect costs. Expenses directly related to growing spinach, such as labor, equipment, seeds, fertilizer, and pesticides, might be considered direct expenditures. Overhead charges for things like electricity, salaries for administrators, and other operational expenditures are examples of indirect costs. Farmers can discover cost-saving options, learn more about the profitability of growing spinach, and make well-informed decisions to allocate resources as efficiently as possible by performing a complete cost analysis.

FINANCIAL PLANNING AND BUDGETING

Financial planning and budgeting are essential to the success of any agricultural endeavor, including spinach growing. A well-organized budget is necessary for controlling spending, effectively allocating resources, and reaching financial objectives. A budget for spinach farming would include expected expenses, income, and cash flow estimates. When creating a budget, farmers must take into account variables including market prices, seasonal fluctuations, and possible dangers. Together with budgeting, financial planning entails defining long-term financial objectives, developing plans for reaching those objectives, and setting up backup plans for unanticipated difficulties. Resilience and sustainability are guaranteed in spinach farming operations through effective financial planning.

OPTIONS FOR FINANCING SPINACH FARMING

If spinach growers want to start or grow their business, one of the most important things they can do is check into financial possibilities. There are numerous funding options available, such as conventional bank loans, grants and subsidies from the government, and private investments. Agribusiness-specific loans may be available from financial institutions, which consider crop cycles and market conditions.

Government initiatives frequently offer grants or subsidies to promote environmentally friendly farming methods. Spinach farming endeavors may also attract the interest of private investors, particularly if they coincide with objectives related to social or environmental effects. Making decisions that support the financial objectives of spinach farming initiatives requires careful evaluation of the terms, interest rates, and repayment schedules of each funding source.

In the context of spinach farming, cost analysis, budgeting, and investigating funding possibilities are essential elements of efficient financial management. Farmers can better understand their financial situation, pinpoint development opportunities, and increase overall profitability by performing a complete cost analysis. While budgeting guarantees effective resource distribution and goal-oriented financial planning, looking into a variety of funding sources supplies the funds required to start or grow spinach farming businesses. A thorough approach to financial management is necessary for spinach farming endeavors to be successful and long-lasting.

CHAPTER NINE

REGULATORY AND LEGAL ASPECTS

COMPREHENDING AGRICULTURAL REGULATIONS

Rules governing agriculture have a significant impact on how the farming sector operates and how its practices are developed. These rules are intended to preserve the entire integrity of the food supply chain, safeguard the environment, and guarantee the safety of agricultural goods. Comprehending the wide array of regulations that oversee different facets of agriculture, such as land utilization, product labeling, and production techniques, is crucial.

These laws are frequently passed by both the federal government and the state governments, creating a complicated web of rules that farmers have to follow. State agriculture departments may enact extra laws specific to their regions, but federal organizations, like the U.S. Department of Agriculture (USDA), provide general guidelines.

To guarantee compliance and steer clear of any legal ramifications, farmers must remain knowledgeable about these requirements.

PERMITS AND LICENSES

One of the most important parts of running a farm legally is getting the required licenses and permissions. Depending on the kind of agricultural operations being engaged, such as crop cultivation, livestock farming, or agribusiness endeavors, different license requirements may apply. To transport goods over state lines, sell specialized items, or operate machinery, farmers can require permits.

Another essential element of agricultural law compliance is permits. For example, actions that could affect the quality of the air or water may need environmental permissions. Zoning permits could also be required to make sure the farm complies with established land use guidelines.

Farming operations may be suspended, fines assessed, or legal action taken if the necessary licenses and permits are not obtained.

ADHERENCE TO ENVIRONMENTAL STANDARDS

The environment may be impacted by agricultural operations in several ways, including emissions, water pollution, and soil erosion. To lessen these effects and preserve sustainable farming methods, compliance with environmental norms is crucial. Environmental rules frequently cover topics including trash disposal, water management, and the use of pesticides.

Farmers must comply with the guidelines established by environmental protection organizations to mitigate any adverse impacts on human health and ecosystems. In addition to ensuring regulatory compliance, putting best practices for integrated pest management, soil conservation, and water conservation into practice helps to assure the long-term sustainability of agricultural operations.

Successfully negotiating the legal and regulatory environment in agriculture demands a thorough comprehension of agricultural laws, persistent work to secure required licenses and permissions, and a dedication to upholding environmental standards. By doing this, farmers may support the resilience and sustainability of the agricultural sector as a whole in addition to avoiding legal issues.